Other books written by this author

-Our Story of a Twin Flame Union

- Akashic Realm Journeys

<u>Dua (Thanks and praises)</u>

Dua Pa Neter, Nebetcher, the Creative force that exist within all things. You are the spark within me that connects us all.

Dua, to my ancestors, who suffered and achieved so much. Without you I wouldn't be here to do what I do now.

Dua, to the Elders, Thank you for sharing your Wisdom and walking your journeys.

Finally, much Thanks to my family who inspire me in all that I do. To my King Uraeus Ophaughnie Neteru Amaru Anuwi Heru-Ur, Thank you for your support always. To my daughters (and any other future children that Will come thru), Maati Takala Merit-Heru and Naeemah Amari Nefertah, may you always know magic in your lives.

Table of Contents

Part 1

-Mythology

-The Calendar Explained

- Solar Calendar

Part 2

-Pronounciation Guide

-Suggested Reading

-Bibliography

Part 1

"Mastery of self consists not in abnormal dreams, visions and fantastic imaginings or living, but in using the higher Forces against the lower, thus escaping the pains of the lower by vibrating on the higher" - Kemetic proverb

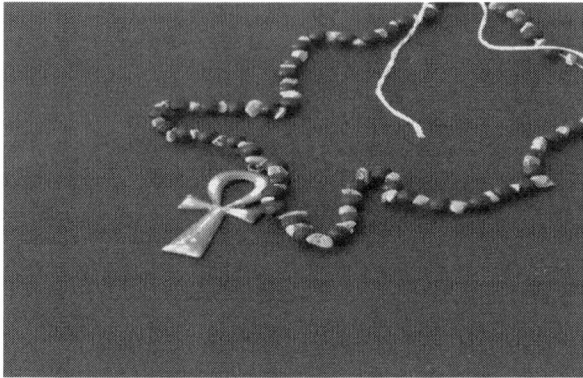

Mythology

In the beginning was the waters of Nun. This vast endless ocean of infinite possibilities flowed. There was a stillness in these waters, as there was nothing to disrupt it. Nun would have continued this way, in it's timeless flow had the first Thump not occurred. Thump, thump, thump was the sound that could be heard rising from the primordial waters. This thumping spread up and turned into the first heartbeat. Like the beating on a drum, Ra emerged from the waters speaking his own name and bringing himself into existence. From Amen (the hidden one) to Ra (the energy of all) the Sun rose over the Blackness of the primordial sea. Our ancestors didn't have a concept of nothingness or zero as all things come from the infinite Nun and return back to its Ether. So you see from infinite creation and possibility comes Ra the first creation.

Ra soon found he wanted to create more beings like him. From the air of Ra's breath emerged Shu and from the moisture of his tongue came Tefnut. Ra was now a father and would never again be alone in Creation. Now there were three elements, fire (Ra), air (Shu), and water (Tefnut). Shu and Tefnut also decided they wanted to help in the making of creation. While Ra spoke things into life (animals and plants) his children Tefnut and Shu became our world's first Divine union. From this union came the first twins Geb (earth) and Nut (sky/ether).

The twins emerged from their mother's womb entwined body to body. Ra could foresee that the earth and sky being joined together, as they were, would cause a problem for his other creations. Ra decreed that Geb and Nut be separated since they refused to do so themselves. This is why there is air that continually rest between the earth and the sky. Shu stands between them so that we can all walk on the land without being crushed by the sky.

Ra had not decreed the separation of Geb and Nut early enough to prevent them from procreating, but in his rage at their defiance, he decided that Nut would not be able to bear her children on any day of the year. At that time the year lasted 360 days. In the meantime Djehuti (the voice and reason of Ra), and Maat (the Neteret of balance, and justice) had been created. Djehuti heard of Ra's scheme to keep Nut from birthing her children and her wails of never ending labor. This disturbed him so much that he came up with an idea on how Nut would be relieved of labor.

Djehuti in the form of the wise and crafty baboon came to Ra and challenged him to a game of dice. They both made small wagers and for a while every game was won by Ra. This built up Ra's confidence. Over time the wagers got bigger and bigger until Djehuti wagered for a day of sunlight. Ra thought over if he was willing to give up some daylight. Since he had won so much he decided to bet the daylight, feeling he was more likely to win over the baboon with bad luck. As Djehuti picked up the dice to throw it he whispered an enchantment over them causing him to win. Djehuti kept winning daylight until he had won enough days to add to the end of the year for each of Geb and Nut's children, that way they could be born on their own days. This is why we have 365 days instead of 360 in each year. Nut celebrates the birth of her five children Ausar, Heru Ur, Setekh, Auset, and Nebt-Hut at the end of each year.

The Calendar explained

The Kemetic people had a calendar of 365 days. There were three seasons with four months in each season (12 months in total). Each month consisted of three ten day weeks (30 days) and each day had a special name for it. There is a 13th month that consist of five days to mark the days Djehuti won for the birth of each of Geb and Nut's children. The beginning of the year was measured by the first sighting of Sopdet (Sirius) in the east rising before the Sun. Depending on where your temple was located this day could vary. The calendar that is in this book was measured the same way by myself. The sighting of Sopdet was measured from Arizona instead of Egypt (as many modern Kemetic Reconstructionist use). I chose to do the measurement from Arizona as this is where my temple is. I used many sources and intuition for the placement of each of the holy days. You will not find another Kemetic temple calendar like this one. You may use this calendar for your own practices, as is, or change what you need to for your practice. Remember this is a Spiritual practice NOT a religion. Where religion stagnates and binds back the Ka (Spirit) and Ba(Soul) from Evolving, whereas Spirituality Does the exact opposite allowing for growth and flow into more living breathing realities. Each of the days listed below starts with the words Heru m meaning Day of (this denotes the day of the month for example Heru m Djehuti is the first day of every month). You will see terms in Medu Neter on this calendar. Ament is to as "the field of reeds". The word Ament will be repeated throughout the Calendar as a representation of the concept of "Heaven".

"Gods are immortal men, and men are mortal Gods"- Kemetic Proverb

Since we are all Divine beings in mortal form it only makes since to celebrate our own births as we do the Neteru. I encourage you to do as my family does. Each month on the number day that each of us were born we do something special to acknowledge the birth of a Neter. If you were born October 15th then the fifteenth of every month would be your holy day. On these holy days, praises, feasts, and offerings are made to your Higher Self. In essence you will be sending Spiritual energy to yourself which can bring you closer to attaining Enlightenment!

*(**Note that anything with a * next to it are events where the dates are likely to change from year to year. Such things are equinoxes, solstices, full moons, new moons, and quarter moons**)*

<u>Sacred names of the days of the month</u>

1) Djehuti
     21) Anpu

2) Heru netchyef
     22) Na

3) Ausar
     23) Na Ur

4) Amset
     24) Na Djesher

5) Hap
     25) Shema

6) Duamutef
     26) Maameref

7)Qebhsenuf
     27) Nut

8)Maatitef-f
     28) Khnemu

9)Arit-tef-ef
     29) Utettefef

10)Arireneftchesef
     30) Nehes

11)Netchetur

12) Netchsnaa

13) Teken

14) Hemba

15) Armauai

16) Mehefkheruf

17) Heruheriuatchf

18) Ahi

19) Anmutef

20) Upuatu

Seasons of the year

Akhet- Innudation

Peret- Emergence

Shemew- Harvest

Special (every changing dates) Days (*on the calendar they are marked with this* *)

Equinox	Solstice	Moons
Spring- Kheper Moon- Aah Nemah	Winter- Nen	New
Fall-Kheper quarter Moon- Deni tep	Summer- Aapi/ Ap	1st
Moon- Aah Meh Utchet		Full
quarter Moon- Anep		3rd

Sacred names of the months of the year and their meanings

Djehuti (Named after Djehuti)

Pa N Ipt (The one of Karnak)

Hut-Heru (Named after Hut-Heru)

Ka He Ka (Soul upon Soul)

Ta Aabt (The offering)

Pa N Pa Mkhru (The one of the censer)

Pa N Imn-Htp (The one of Amenhotep)

Pa N Rnnwtt (The one of Rennutet)

Pa N Khsw (The one of Khonsu)

Pa N Int (The one of the Wodi)

Ipy Ipy (Selected)

Mswt-Re (Birth of Ra)

Hery W Rnpt (the month of the birth of Nut and Gebs children)

Meswt Ausar (Birth of Ausar)

Meswt Heru UR (Birth of Heru Ur)

Meswt Setekh (Birth of Setekh)

Meswt Auset (Birth of Auset)

Meswt Nebt-Hut (Birth of Nebt-Hut)

Dates of the moon cycles 7/27/2019-7/27/2020

New moon- 7/31, 8/30, 9/28, 10/27, 11/26, 12/25, 1/24, 2/23, 3/24, 4/22, 5/22, 6/20, 7/20

1st quarter moon- 8/7, 9/5, 10/5, 11/4, 12/3, 1/2, 2/1, 3/2, 4/1, 4/30, 5/29, 6/28

Full Moon- 8/15, 9/13, 10/13, 11/12, 12/11, 1/10, 2/9, 3/9, 4/7, 5/7, 6/5, 7/4

3rd quarter moon-8/23, 9/21, 10/21, 11/19, 12/18, 1/17, 2/15, 3/16, 44/14, 5/14, 6/12, 7/12

Dates of the moon cycles 7/27/2020-7/27/2021

New moon-8/18, 9/17, 10/16, 11/14, 12/14, 1/12, 2/11, 3/13, 4/11, 5/11, 6/10, 7/9

1st quarter moon- 7/27, 8/25, 9/23, 10/23, 11/21, 12/21, 1/20, 2/19, 3/21, 4/20, 5/19, 6/17, 7/17

Full moon-8/3/, 9/1, 10/1, 10/31, 11/30, 12/29, 1/28, 2/27, 3/28, 4/26, 5/26, 6/24, 7/23

3rd quarter moon- 8/11, 9/10, 10/9, 11/8, 12/7, 1/6, 2/4, 3/5, 4/4, 5/3, 6/2, 7/1

Pr Nehast

(Solar Calendar 7/2018-7/2019)

<u>Season of Akhet, Month of Djehuti</u>

Heru m Djehuti 7/27 -Heru n tep renpet (New Year's Day), Feast of Djehuti

*Aah meh utchet (full moon)

Heru m HeruNetchtef 7/28- Temple cleansing

Heru m Ausar- Feast of Akhet

Heru m Duamutef 8/1- Festival of Opet and the rise of the Nile waters

Heru m Qebhsenuf 8/2- The temple Neteru go before Ra

Heru m Aritchetef 8/4-

*Anep (third quarter moon)

Heru m Arireneftchesef 8/5- Neteru are peaceful stearing Ra's sky boat on course

Heru m Netchsnaa 8/7- Rise of Nile with offerings to Neteru

Heru m Hemba 8/9- Day when the heart is at peace

Heru m Armauai 8/10- Festival of Hedj-Hotep in honor of the Neteret (Goddess) of weaving

Heru m Mehefkheruf 8/11- Feast of Nut and Ra

*Aah Nema (New moon)

Heru m Naur 8/18- Festival establishing Heru as king

Heru m Nadjesher 8/19- Feast to temple Neteru, incesence are burned as an offering

Heru m Maameref 8/21- Offerings to temple Neteru

Heru m Khnemu 8/23- Day of battle between Heru and Setekh

Heru m Utettefef 8/24- Ra journys accross the Skys

Heru m Nehes 8/25- Day Setekhs army's didnt triumph, dont go out after sundown, Feast day in the temples of Heru, Ra, and Ausar

Month of Pa Nipt

Heru M Djehuti 8/26- Feast of Hapi

    * Aah meh Utchet (full moon)

Heru m HeruNetchetf 8/27- Day of peace between Heru and Setekh

Heru m Asar 8/28- The sight of Heru and Setekh pleases the Neteru

Heru m Qebhsenuf 9/1- Heru-Ur travels to Nut. This is a day of offering to the Neteru

Heru m Maati-tafuf 9/2- Djehuti Heals the eye of Heru

    * Anep (third quarter moon)

Heru m Arireneftchesef 9/4- Birth of Geb and Nut

Heru m Nechetur 9/5- Harmony in Ament All Neteru Celebrate

Heru m Netchsnaa 9/6- Birth of Hut-Heru

Heru m Armauai 9/9- Procession of Bastet

*Aah Nema- New moon

Heru m Mehefkheruf 9/10- Day Ra judges the dispute between Setekh and Heru

Heru m Ahi 9/12- Feast for the Neteru

Heru m Anmutef 9/13- Day Heru is given the white crown. The black land is given to Heru, The red land is given to Setekh

Heru m Anpu 9/15- Feast day of Ausar

Heru m Na 9/16- Day of offerings to the Neteru

*Deni tep- 1st quarter moon

Heru m Shema 9/20- Birth of Bastet

Heru m Khnemu 9/22-

*Kheper (fall equinox)

Heru m Nehes 9/24- Feast day in the temples of the Neteru

*Aah Meh Utchet-Full moon

Month of Hut-Heru

Heru m Duamutef 9/30- Feast day for Hut-Heru (a day to commemorate love)

Heru m Maatitef-f 10/2-

*Anep - 3rd quarter moon

Heru m Netchetur 10/5- Day to give thanks to the Neteru of the two lands

Heru m Hemba 10/8-

*Aah Nema - New moon

Heru m Armauai 10/9-Day of rejoice in Ament (a good day for field/garden work)

Heru m Heruheriuatchf 10/11- Day of peace, eye of Heru returns to Ra

Heru m Anpu 10/15- Day of eternal happiness, all Neteru celebrate

Heru m Na 10/16-

> * Deni Tep - 1st quarter moon

Heru m Maameref 10/20 - The feast of Shu

Heru m Nut 10/21- Day of raising the image of Maat before Ra

Heru m Utettefef 10/23- Festival of Selket (scorpion Neteret)

Heru m Nehes 10/24- Feast day in the temples of Heru, Ausar, and Ra

> *Aah Meh Utchet (full moon)

Month of Ka he Ka

Heru m Amset 10/28- Feast of Sobek

Heru m Duamutef 10/30- Ra is joyful. This is a day of fertility and the creative power of Nun is in all.

Heru m Qebhsenuf 10/31- All Neteru Rejoice

> *Anep- 3rd quarter moon

Heru m Aritchetef 11/2- Temple rituals and offerings to Sobek

Heru m Hemba 11/7- Djehuti and Neteru cause defeat of Setekh, avoid hard tasks today

> *Aah Nema- New moon

Heru m Mehefkheruf 11/9- Day of the feast of the resurrection of Ausar, the ancestors rejoice.

Heru m Ahi 11/11- Day of going forth of Hut-heru. (Day of rest no working. day of solitude)

Heru m Upuatu 11/13- Feast day of Bastet and Sekhmet

Heru m Anpu 11/14-

* Deni tep- 1st quarter moon

Heru m Khnemu 11/21- The day the enemies of Heru try to kill him, stay indoors at night

Heru m Utettefef 11/22-

* Aah Meh Utchet- Full moon

Heru m Nehes 11/23- Feast day in the temples of Ra, Heru, and Ausar

Season of Peret, Month of Ta Aaht

Heru m Duamutef 11/29- Double offerings and gifts to Neb-Kau (Neter of Ka)

Heru m Qebhsenuf 11/30- Day of Rest

Heru m Netchetur 12/4- Double offerings made to Wepwat and Ausar (good day for furthering ambitions)

Heru m Hemba 12/7- Feast of beer and cakes for Sekhmet also for other Neteru

*Aah Nema-New moon

Heru m Ahi 12/11- Day for praying for long life and praises to Maat in the temples

Heru m Upuatu 12/13- Going forth of Nun and all the Primordial Neteru

Heru m Anpu 12/14- Day Shu sends good dry air to the ancestors in honor. (Ancestor honor day)

Heru m Na 12/15-

*Deni Tep- 1st quarter moon

Heru m Na Ur 12/16- Going forth of the Neteru to the city Ausar rules in

Heru m Maameref 12/19- Day Bastet guards the two lands. (Make offerings to the Neteru)

Heru m Khnemu 12/21- Silent night (Day of fasting, chanting, meditation and reflection)

*Nen- Winter Solstice

Heru m Utettefef 12/22- Silent night (Day of fasting, chanting, meditation and reflection) Earth and Ament in harmony

*Aah Meh Utchet-Full moon

Heru m Nehes 12/23- Silent night (Day of fasting, chanting, meditation and reflection; offerings of incense to all the Neteru). Day Ra banishes Geb from Nut (Don't drink cow's milk today in honor of Nut the Heavenly Cow)

Month of Pa N Pa Mkheru

Heru m Djehuti 12/24- Silent night (Day of fasting, chanting, meditation and reflection)

Heru m Herunetchtef 12/25- Birth of Heru Sa Auset (Heru son of Auset). Festival of Ra's emergence from the dark, so he may gain strength in the coming month.

Heru m Ausar 12/26- Day Djehuti renews his allegiance to Ra. Day of rest and Jubilation.

Heru m Amset 12/27- Bastet and Sekhmet guard the two lands, all Neteru are happy

Heru m Duamutef 12/29-Day of celebrating the architect of the world Ptah (he lifts Manu with his two hands).

*Anep-3rd quarter moon

Heru m Qebhsenuf 12/30- The day the Neteru receive Ra, Everything in the universe is in a state of Maat

Heru m Aritchetef 1/1- Festival to great ancestors. Pay homage to your ancestors

Heru m Netchsnaa 1/4- A day of offering to Akhu (ancestors) and Neteru

Heru m Teken 1/5-

*Aah Nema- New moon

Heru m Mehefkheruf 1/8- Feast day of Neith and the making of oracles.

Heru m Anmutef 1/11- The day Ra escapes Apep with the help of Setekh who guards the heavenly boat in the Duat.

Heru m Upuatu 1/12- Neteru pay tribute to Ra on his safe return. Ra pays tribute to Ausar and offers him the Ankh and scepter.

Heru m Anpu 1/13- Day Auset obtains Ra's secret name, and power over creation. Day Heru defeats Setekh.

*Deni tep- 1St quarter moon

Heru m Na 1/14- Day of respect for the organs of Ausar that have been placed in the hands of Anpu for preservation.

Heru m Maameref 1/18- A day of the receiving of wealth (a good day to take inventory)

Heru m Khnemu 1/20-

* Aah Meh Utchet- Full moon

Heru m Nehes 1/22- Feast day in the temples of Ra, Heru, and Ausar

Month of Pa N Imn-Htp

Heru m Djehuti 1/23- Going forth of Min (a day of copulation and fertility)

Heru m Ausar 1/25- Ausar is pleased, the spirits of the dead rejoice

Heru m Hap 1/27-

* Anep- 3rd quarter moon

Heru m Duamutef 1/28- Celebration of the unification of the two lands. Heru is celebrated.

Heru m Arireneftchesef 2/1- Neith goes forth to Sais; her beauty is shown to all. (Do not copulate this night)

Heru m Netchetur 2/2- Festival of rebirth. The going forth of Anpu and his embalmers that receive everyone upon death.

Heru m Teken 2/4- Khnum makes ready the emergence of the Neteru

*Aah Nema-New moon

Heru m Hemba 2/5- Day of Judgment and purification

Heru m Mehefkheruf 2/7- Day of the dead. Dead go through all the cities of the dead (graveyards) and fight off Apep. Dead imbue the living with protection.

Heru m Heruheriuatchf 2/8- The day the waters of Hapi come from the waters of Nun. Hapi brings joy and food. Food offerings are made.

Heru m Ahi 2/9- Day Djehuti and his spirits go forth. Great day for magic.

Heru m Anpu 2/12-

> * Deni Tep-1st quarter moon

Heru m Naur 2/14- Feast day for Nut

Heru m Khnemu 2/19-

> *Aah Meh Utchet- Full moon

Heru m Nehes 2/21- Feast day in the temples of Ra, Ausar, Heru. Feast day and promise of immortality

Month of Pa N Rnnwtt

Heru m Ausar 2/24- Feast day for Ausar

Heru m Hap 2/26-

> *Anep- 3rd quarter moon

Heru m Duamutef 2/27- Day enemies of Auset are defeated. Great feast in Ament.

Heru m Qebhsenuf 2/28- Day priest of Geb go to see Anpu and talk of requirements (the tombs to be set)

Heru m Aritchetef 3/2- All Neteru satisfied. Everything is in its place in Ament.

Heru m Netchetur 3/5- Day of going forth of Min, Day of lovemaking and fertility. Incense offering of Myrrh made.

Heru m Teken 3/6-The eye of Heru is in its place. All parts are accounted for. The Neteru are joyous.

*Aah Nemah- New moon

Heru m Armauai 3/8- The complete eye of Heru is introduced to the Neteru. Ra's power strengthens the Neteru.

Heru m Upuatu 3/13- Day of happiness for Neteru of Eastern horizon. All Neteru rejoice.

Heru m Anpu 3/14- Going forth of Kephera all people rejoice

*Deni tep

Heru m Nadjesher 3/17- Day Ra travels across Ament. Feast day for all Neteru.

Heru m Nut 3/20-

*Kheper- Spring equinox

*Aah Meh Utchet- Full moon

Heru m Nehes 3/23- Feast day in the temples of Heru, Auasar, Ra. Offerings made to Ptah, Sokar, Ausar, Ra and any personal temple Neteru

Season of Shemew, Month of Pa N Khonsu

Heru m Amset 3/27-The Neteru are satisfied and warship Ausar. Incense myrrh and offerings made to local Neteru.

*Anep- 3rd quarter moon

Heru m Duamutef 3/29- Feast day of heru

Heru m Netchetur 4/3-The great Neteru come forth from the house of Ra and receive the eye of Heru.

Heru m Netchsnaa 4/4- The day Heru defeats his enemy Setekh. The ancestors look on and every heart is happy.

Heru m Teken 4/5-

>*Aah Nemah- New moon

Heru m Upuatu 4/12-

>*Deni tep- 1st quarter moon

Heru m Naur 4/15- Day the Neteru and ancestors rejoice

Heru m Nadjesher 4/16- All Neteru Rejoyce, this is the day Djehuti heard Maat

Heru m Shema 4/17- 1st day of Sokar festival commemorating Ausars death

Heru m Maameref 4/18- 2nd day of Sokar festival, Auset grieves the loss of her husband

Heru m Nut 4/19-3rd day of Sokar festival, Auset, Nebt-Hut, Anpu look for the body of Ausar

Heru m Khnemu 4/20- 4th day of Sokar festival, Auset finds pillar in king's palace

Heru m Utetteff 4/21- 5th day of Sokar festival, Ausar is resurrected (Auset rejoices and becomes pregnant)

Heru m Nehes 4/22- Feast day in the temples of Heru, Ausar, Ra. Raising of the Djed Pillar.

Month of Pa N Int

Heru m Amset 4/26-

>*Anep- 3rd quarter moon

Heru m Qebhsenuf 4/29- The Neteru in the sun boat of Ra are in Festivity.

Heru m Maatiteff 4/30- Feast day in Ament and Ta (Heaven and Earth)

Heru m Netchsnaa 5/4-

> *Aah Nemah- New moon

Heru m Teken 5/5- Feast day for Ra and the Neteru of Ament

Heru m Hemba 5/6- Offerings of sweet herbs and incense made to please Ra

Heru m Ahi 5/10- Feast of Wadjet. A day of singing and chanting. Offerings of sweet herbs and incense made.

Heru m Anmutef 5/11-

> *Deni tep- 1st quarter moon

Heru m Maameref 5/18-

> *Aah Meh Utchet- Full moon

Heru m Nehes 5/22- Feast day in the temples of Heru, Ra, Ausar. Day all are made happy by the eye of Heru.

Month of Ipy Ipy

Heru m Ausar 5/25- Day of purification of the Neteru, Ausar worshipped with offerings

Heru m Amset 5/26-

> *Anep-3rd quarter moon

Heru m Duamutef 5/28- Day of celebration with Hut-Heru

Heru m Qebhsenuf 5/29- Feast day for all Neteru

Heru m Netchsnaa 6/3-

*Aah Nemah- New moon

Heru m Hemba 6/5- Feast day for all Neteru. Peace declared after Sekhmet wakes from night of bear and cakes.

Heru m Heruheriuatchf 6/8- The reception of Ra. Day of celebration for everyone.

Heru m Ahi 6/9-

*Deni tep-1st quarter moon

Heru m Upuatu 6/11- Heru hears the words of the people in the presence of the Neteru.

Heru m Maameref 6/17-

*Aah Meh Utchet- Full moon

Heru m Nehes 6/21- Feast day in temples of Heru, Ra, Ausar. Setekh goes forth at noon (don't travel outside at noon).

*Aapi- Summer solstice

Month of Meswt Ra

Heru m Amset 6/25- Festival of Mut offerings made in her honor

*Anep- 3rd quarter moon

Heru m Duamutef 6/27- Offerings made to all those in Ament. Neteru have a feast for Ausar.

Heru m Qebhsenuf 6/28- Day Maat and all Neteru perform all proper rituals, the universe in in harmony.

Heru m Arireneftchesef 7/1- Temple festivals. Min copulates with Akmim. A day for conceiving children.

Heru m Netchetur 7/2-

*Aah Nemah- New moon

Heru m Armauai 7/6- Day Setekh Attacks Ra at sunrise and loses. Good fortune comes at sunrise.

Heru m Heruheriuatchf 7/8- Victory celebration through3out all the land. All Neteru are happy.

Heru m Ahi 7/9- Auset defends Heru against Setekh

*Deni tep- 1st quarter moon

Heru m Anpu 7/12- Day of libation offerings for ancestors.

Heru m Nadjesher 7/15- Feast day in honor of local Neteru

Heru m Shema 7/16-

*Aah Meh Utchet- Full moon

Heru m Maameref 7/17- Neteru sail to make the waters of Hapi rise, do not venture out at noon.

Heru m Nut 7/18- Feast day for Anpu, the Neteru purify themselves today.

Heru m Khnemu 7/19- Feast day for Min, Day of fertility.

Month of Hery W Rnpt

(Each day is filled with festivities for the birth of the Neter of the day offerings are made)

Meswt Ausar 7/22- Birth of Ausar

Meswt Heru UR 7/23- Birth of Heru Ur

Meswt Setekh 7/24- Birth of Setekh

*Anep- 3rd quarter moon

Meswt Auset 7/25- Birth of Auset

Meswt Nebt-Hut 7/26- Birth of Nebt-Hut

Part 2

"If Mind and Divine speech are used as meant, you will not differ from the immortals in any way"- Kemetic proverb

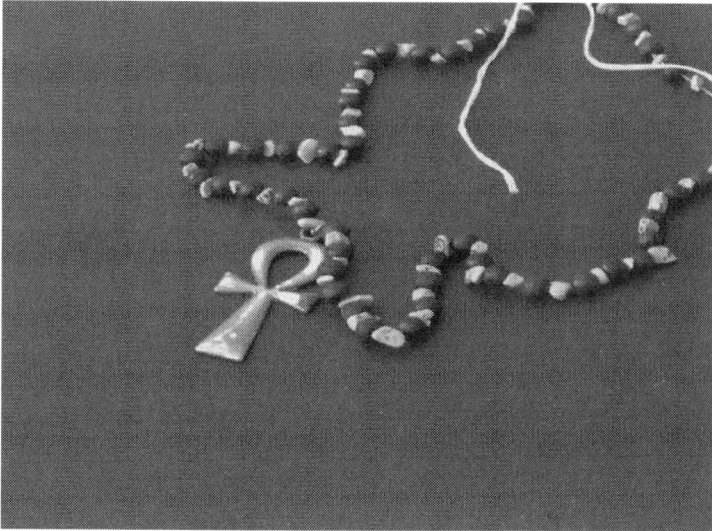

Pronounciation Guide

Sacred names of the days of the month

1) Djehuti-(Je who tee)

2) Heru netchyef- (Hair oo net ch ee ef)

3) Ausar- (Ah-sar)

4) Amset- (Ahm set)

5) Hap- (Hah p)

6) Duamutef- (Do ah moot ef)

7)Qebhsenuf- (Kebh sen oof)

8)Maatitef-f-(May aht ee tef f)

9)Arit-tef-ef- (Areet tef ef)

10)Arireneftchesef-(Aree- ren ef ch es ef)

11)Netchetur- (Net-ch et er)

12) Netchsnaa- (Net-ch sen ay)

13) Teken- (Tech-en)

14) Hemba- (Hem bah)

15) Armauai- (Arma oo ah ee)

16) Mehefkheruf-(Meh ef ker oof)

17) Heruheriuatchf- (Hair oo hair ee ooah t ch ef)

18) Ahi-(Ee he)

19) Anmutef - (Ahn moot ef)

20) Upuatu- (Oop oo ah too)

21) Anpu- (Ahn poo/ in poo)

22) Na- (nay)

23) Na Ur- (Nay er)

24) Na Djesher- (Nay je sher)

25) Shema- (she mah)

26) Maameref- (Mah mer ef)

27) Nut- (Noot)

28) Khnemu- (Kh nem oo)

29) Utettefef- (Oot et ef ef)

30) Nehes- (Nee-hes)

Seasons of the year

Akhet- (akh-et)

Peret- (per-ett)

Shemew- (shem-ee-oo)

Special (every changing dates) Days (*on the calendar they are marked with this **)

Equinox's/Solstices

Kheper-(Ke-per)

Nen- (Nen)

Aapi/ Ap- (Ay ah pee/ Ah p)

Moons

Aah Nemah (Ee-ay-h Nee-mah)

Deni tep- (Den ee tep)

Aah Meh Utchet- (Ee-ay-h meh oot ch et)

Anep- (Ah nep)

Sacred names of the months of the year and their meanings

Djehuti- (Je who tee)

Pa N Ipt- (Pa en I-pet)

Hut-Heru- (hut hair-oo)

Ka He Ka- (Kah hee kah)

Ta Aabt- (Tah ay ah-bet)

Pa N Pa Mkhru- (Pah en pah mmk hair-oo)

Pa N Imn-Htp- (Pah en i-men hoe-tep/ Pah en Amen hoe-tep)

Pa N Rnnwtt- (Pah en Ren-wet/ Pah en Ren-oot)

Pa N Khsw- (Pah en Kh-sue)

Pa N Int- (Pah en Int)

Ipy Ipy- (Ip-ee ip-ee)

Meswt-Re - (Mes oot Ra/ Mes oot Ray)

Hery W Rnpt- (Hairy w Ren-pet)

Meswt Ausar-(Mes oot Ah-sar)

Meswt Heru UR-(Mes oot Hair-oo Er/ Mes oot Hair-oo Wer)

Meswt Setekh -(Mes oot See-tech)

Meswt Auset -(Mes oot Ah-set)

Meswt Nebt-Hut - (Mes oot Neb et Hut)

Names of the Neteru (*In no particular order*)

Aset- (Ah-set) also known as Isis or Ast

Ausar- (Ah-sar) also known as Osiris or Asar

Ra- (Rah, Ray) also known as Re

Nun- (Noon)

Tefnut- (Tef- noot)

Shu- (Shoe)

Anpu- (Ahn- poo/ In-poo) also known as Anubis

Min- (Men)

Geb- (Geb)

Nut-(Noot)

Maat-(May-aht)

Setekh- (See-tech) also known as Set or Seth

Djehuti- (Je-who-tee) also known as Tehuti or Thoth

Heru- (Hair-oo) also known as Horus

Heru Sa Auset- (Hair-oo Sah Ah-set) Heru son of Auset

Heru Ur- (Hair-oo Er/ Hair-oo Wer) Heru the elder the brother of Auset and Ausar not the son

Nebet-Hut- (Ne-bet Hut) also known as Nebthys

Hut-Heru- (Hut Hair-oo) also known as Hathor

Bastet- (Bah-stet) also known as Bast

Sekhmet-(Seckh- met)

Sobek- (So-beck) also known as Sebek

Apep- (Ah-pep)

<u>Other Miscellaneous words</u>

Sokar-(So-car)

Opet- (Oh-pet)

Akhu- (Ah kh-oo)

Ammit- (Ah-mmit)

Sopdet- (So ped et)

Suggested Reading

-Seeded Ascension by: Uraeus Ophaughnie Neteru Amaru Anuwi

-Egyptian Proverbs compiled by :Muata Abhaya Ashby

-Bhakti Yoga: The yoga of love and divotion by Swami Vivekananda

-Devotional Worship book of Shetaut Neter by: Muata Ashby

(and)

All other Kemetic books soon to come by Ayeri Nyah Assom

Bibliography

Isis: Queen of Egyptian magic by: Jonathan Dee

Ancient Egyptian Divination and Magic by: Eleanor L. Harris

An Egyptian Hierogylphic Dictionary volume 1&2 by: E.A Wallis
Budge

Egyptian Magic by: E. A. Wallis Budge

Sesh Medew Netcher: A beginner's introduction to medew
netcher by : Wudjau Men-ib Iry-Maat

Kemetictemple.org

Made in the USA
Monee, IL
01 July 2021